Faces of
Womanhood

Faces of Womanhood

a poetry anthology

blood moon POETRY

.

For all women:
written by we, who know us best of all.

Note from the Editor

blood moon POETRY was co-founded in the midst of great social upheaval, a time when we were collectively facing one of the greatest challenges of our lifetime. I was also a first time (and very new) mama. During both a global pandemic and my experience with postnatal depression, writing poetry became a way to ground myself while the storm raged in the outer—and my inner—world.

My co-founder, Monica, and I made an instant connection on Instagram, the platform we both used to share our poems with a community of women and mothers who also happened to be poets. Both of us raising girls in a world we found more terrifying than ever, yet finding solace in words scribbled in the chaste, stolen moments most working mothers come to cherish.

Working with only small windows of time that closed very quickly, it was almost impossible to navigate the various publications accepting submissions. I had already had a collection of my poems published in the book *Not The Only One* and in various zines and indie magazines but was looking to make the big leap into journals.

In the last VIDA count, only three publications published 50% or more women and non-binary writers, an increase of just one literary magazine since their last main count in 2017, which found women writers' work made up just under 40% of publications. Poetry presses are largely still highlighting men's voices in a world where, arguably, what we need now more than ever is to hear what women have to say.

blood moon POETRY was born from a shared desire to find, nurture, and expose the poetic work of women whose voices would otherwise go unheard. We work only with women illustrators and designers, and our editorial board has always been a mix of women who share our ethos. Our submission process is open, simple, and transparent with our mission to make it as easy as possible for female poets to gain that all-important publication credit. We strive to be welcoming and inclusive, a safe place for all women to gently set down their words.

What you will find here, in the pages of our first print anthology, is a collection of 50 poems written by the women in our Instagram community. "The Faces of Womanhood" began life as an online community project in celebration of International Women's Day 2021. Darci Walker, who started the project on behalf of blood moon, was humbled by the sheer volume of responses written by women all over the world. They were asked to share what they thought the face of womanhood looked like for them, and we were overwhelmed and deeply moved by their poetry. So much so, that Monica and I made the decision to collect together 50 that would become *Faces of Womanhood*.

We hope you come back to this book again and again, searching for new faces or perhaps recognising one or two from your own life experience. Intended to be a celebration of the complex facets of contemporary womanhood, what these poems also do is weave in stories and struggles that have spanned decades yet (sadly) remain as relevant as ever.

Faces of Womanhood is a shout in the dark and a hand firmly clasped. It is the start of a conversation that we encourage you to continue and, if this comes in the form of a poem, we can't wait to read what you have to say.

All proceeds from this anthology will be donated to Womankind Worldwide (www.womankind.org.uk) and Women for Afghan Women (www.womenforafghanwomen.org).

Lunar love,

Holly
Editor & Co-Founder
blood moon POETRY
www.bloodmoonpoetry.com

Foreword

I met Holly Ruskin in a manner that typifies 2020. We met online in the middle of the coronavirus pandemic through a mutual friend who was sure we'd have plenty in common. She was right! Holly came into my life at the perfect time, as I was then writing my first book Not The Only One, which is a collection of real stories from parents who have struggled with their mental health since giving birth. Holly and I had both suffered with postnatal depression and spoke at length about our experiences and how that had influenced our creative output. Holly is a teacher and freelance writer and I am a songwriter for Grammy and Emmy winners, so we both knew the pressures of having our "creative time" invaded by our newborns! Holly wrote her story to be included in the book and then mentioned that she'd written poems about her experiences, which I asked to read, then wept as I absorbed every word she had chosen in each poem. It was as if she had reached into my own experiences and given words to exactly how I had felt during the early days of motherhood. At that moment I knew that these beautiful poems just had to be included in my book and luckily Holly agreed. I'm certain Holly's poems played a huge part in the book becoming an Amazon bestseller in November 2020.

Holly and I spoke about future plans and she revealed that she'd love to collate poems by female writers to encourage their voices and put their work into the world but that she was nervous to make a start on this idea. Thankfully Holly and her co-founder Monica found the courage to do so and I am so delighted that they did as we now have a beautiful collection of poems to dive into.

Faces of Womanhood, is a collection of poems written by the women poets in the blood moon Instagram community and are written about the complex but beautiful topic of the different and personal descriptions of womanhood.

Certain words and terms are hard to define. Oscar Wilde did say, "To define is to limit." And there is one term in particular that seems to have more than one definition—womanhood. When I was named a Woman Of The Year 2020, I was honoured but also challenged by what that title meant. Was it about embracing who you are or displaying the traits deemed ideal in a woman and if so, what are they?

Womanhood is something that I have always found hard to put into words and yet, these incredible female poets have managed to do just that in their own unique voices. Delving into this book has been an education for me.

I was deeply challenged by "Privileged Woman" by Meghana

Manusanipalli, as I'm sure you will be, as so many women are made to feel that we deserve appalling treatment from men simply for being "a woman." The final lines of Ebony Gilbert's spot-pickingly honest poem felt like a perfect way to describe many incredible women I've had the honour to know "she is grit and grace."

There is so much joy and positivity in these pages, one particular line being "watch as we applaud and celebrate one another" from "We Are Diamonds" by Micah Klassen, but also much tenacity, grace, strength and respect pouring from each poem.

The interpretations by each poet of contemporary womanhood are as varied as they are fascinating. Prepare to be moved, challenged, and set free by the searing honesty of these female poets.

Reading this book feels like a gift to myself as I found that I was revealed in these pages. I absorbed, wept over, and smiled at the well-chosen words. When I finished the last page I felt I understood the term "womanhood" so much better and in turn will be able to teach my young daughter about what is means to be a woman.

It's a book I will return to time and again, with a cup of tea and a huge sense of pride in what Holly and these incredible women have put out into the world.

Rachel Walker Mason BCAa
Multi Award Winning Songwriter
Woman Of The Year 2020
Author of Amazon bestseller *Not The Only One*

Table of Contents

The Wheels Just Keep on Turning

I am getting on this train,
stepping over the gap
in pay, in memory. They say
confidence works pretty well,
that the modern woman should know
how to make one good cocktail,
dress for her body type,
have a mouth full of kindness,
assemble furniture, birth a whole
house of beautiful things.

Look how I've become
the station for so many engines
the luck made with just a hex
key. It seems unlocking
a life takes a bunch of women
who are all me. It's true someone
is always needing and I am good
for it.

All I know is there are days
when I cannot do anything
right. And yet,
the hours only go
as far as I take them.

Katy Luxem

Instinct

My Mother always told me never to ignore a hunch.
That pea under the mattress,
        a tingling nerve ending folded inward,
daring your intuition.
A deafening blare from an unphased foghorn.
How to fix something you cannot deem tangible?
Just like the lost shape of you,
the smudged outline of her.

When my Grandmother speaks
she does so by accident, spilling.
Her lips a careless dam to a honeyed reservoir,
filter gushed away
by power of relentless devotion,
not stopping to revise
her innate response, reminding me to use my own,
        to check under the mattress.

It is always enough. Enough
to make you check the map, grip the back
of the passenger seat and twist your glance
to reverse, hoping you do not meet traffic.

When you look to your daughter, tell her,
you are always enough, enough to read a map,
enough to ignore it.

Zara Al-Noah

17

Self Portrait

I look at her
Who is she
This woman
That I criticise
The one with the scars
From picking her spots
Dimply thighs
And deep brown eyes

I poke
the ripply contour
Of her belly overhanging
Judge the anchor shapes
On her chest
Like a mean girl
Bitchy face scanning

Her mouth
is slightly wonky
Her skin is lined
And dry
And she no longer
Has a gap
Anywhere near
Those thighs

The teeth need whitening
The bum tightening
The hips could do
with more curve
I stand back
Take another selfie
That I carefully observe

I look into those
Lovely eyes
That have bravely
Stared grief in the face
That have closed
with exhaustion
But never given up
Wept for the human race

They've sobbed with joy
Dilated in shock
Sparkled
at Christmas lights

Forget windows
to the soul
These are skylights

There are skylights
I look at her mouth
Her pink little mouth
That has sung lullaby
after lullaby
Has kissed with heat
Reassured
Bravely testified

I gaze at her hands
Those chapped
beautiful hands
That once held
a rattle in glee
That have reached out
Helped others up
Written poetry

That belly of hers
She hates so much
That grew and birthed
Her boy
The breasts that fed
Her prem baby
And got her in Playboy

A slightly different
Pale yellow light
Is streaming
Onto her face
She touches her skin
Her identical twin
She is grit and grace

Ebony Gilbert

I Scour Old Photo Albums for Reminders I Am Whole

We may never get everyone to look at the camera
and someone is always blinking,
but when the women in my family gather for a photo
you can trace laugh lines through four generations.

There will be no perfectly posed symmetry
as we cram together like a group hug to fit the frame,
edges slightly blurred.

Years later we'll play *I spy*, searching for items like
wooden spoons and glasses of wine or playing cards we held tight
as we rushed together from all corners of the house
because when someone calls we find ourselves by their side

and it's that fierce sort of tenderness you can see
in the way our arms wrap around each other
that spills out of a memory
to be passed down in stories and celebrations
or sits hand in hand, hearts breaking, at hospital bedsides

I see myself in them long before I ever find where I'm actually standing
in the stubborn jut of a chin, a mischievous smile,
in a love that's so loud a picture speaks.

Jaimee Boake

Women Who Write

We spin stories, twisting together
threads of images, sounds, and feelings
that we weave into word form.
Counting syllables instead of stitches,
we reshuffle, choosing carefully,
the pattern and the rhythm of our craft.

It's pleasant to hear the hum and thrum
of others at work, as we create together, alone.
We pause to admire and inspire, both,
as one of us finishes.

We try on wares, yours and mine,
cloaking our nakedness with warmth
and sometimes understanding,
freely offered to anyone
who also feels the cold.
I'm grateful for space, shared
with women who write.

Kara Simons

I Am Wild Woman

allow me to *gather your bones*
as I sing over them softly
speaking in potent language
once forgotten but being remembered
and build a fire of fervor to heat your humanity
next to the river under the river that never dies

close your eyes and *listen*
to synchronistic sounds that have soothed
and gestated effulgent generations
open your eyes and *see*
count the stars of the spirits
that have been and watch
the seedlings of souls yet to be

feel the matrilineal melody and *dance*
through shadow and light
on the banks of dauntless dreams
where vast captivating currents flash
fluid bodies of ancestral intuitive knowing
as each drop of our individual divine
becomes one

follow the wild call and *return*
through the prismatic portals
that cast rainbows across
the significant space
where your soul stretches
connecting you to the infinite
web of wise women who lovingly hold
the invisible living threads of existence
together and weave tapestries
with immaculate hands

expand your mind and *remember*
all the faces of womanhood
that are embodied within your marrow
and hang on the walls of your heart
ever imprinted upon your molecular makeup
are musings of maidens, mothers and elders
constructing you into a monument of art

stir the celestial cauldron and *create*
concoctions of distilled constellations
and cycles that you crave in your core
drink them down with fascination
while the drumming magnetic moon

calls you from your cryptic cloudy chrysalis
into reconfigured redolent freedom

if you forget your power, *do not fear*
my footsteps wait for you to follow
back to the undying mystical flames
of transformation and talismanic truths
transcribed in sagacious telepathy
I cannot be contained by you or me
I only live inside we

I am the archaic anomaly
that dwells
in your abstract arteries

I am the timeless treasury
that remembers faces of the feminine
in her every form

I am the carrier of stories
that compose
your miraculous memoir

I am ceremonial sovereignty that rides
the wind between liminal worlds
and calls you home

Jessamy Joy

The Magic Kingdom

ice cream drips down my chin as we wave
at princesses in a cavalcade, wigs on-point
and on tight, teeth white—did i brush today?
wipe sweat from my brow and hold a grubby
hand. we are all working hard. behind them
a woman in blue pinstripes sweeps, smiling
sweet at a little girl asking *are you cinderella
before?* before answering *no, i'm the fairy
godmother in disguise.* her eyes go wide.

then who am i? dishevelled snack envoy—
footman or royal horse? no.   i am
what we all are: the princess and the fairy.
the wolf and the dragon.

Adrienne K. Burris

The God Story

when you were small you asked me—
mumma, what is God
your kind and gentle heart
so full of wonder and hope
I enfolded you in my arms and
whispered magic into your ears—
God is the deepest mirror
caught in every atom of being
hungry for its own reflection,
creating stars and whale-song
to see its many beautiful faces
whole and miraculous and complete.
That from the stillness of one velvety night
in an outpouring of poetry and art
Woman became and she made Home
and God could finally rest
knowing the future of everything
that truly mattered, is loved and treasured
would be safe within Her light,
birthed and held sacred by this One
we will always return to and
can never lose our hunger to know

Karen Fraser

The Faces of Womanhood

I looked for the faces
The faces of womanhood—
Searching through boxes and drawers
full of memories, stopping to pause
as each came into view, all these women I knew,
all the monochrome mothers, the sepia sisterhood,
Searching for one that would
sum up my sex, be a shining example,
The ultimate sample of all that is womanly,
How would I ever be
able to choose one?

I thought of the faces
I'd known through the decades—
The women I'd lost
though the memory never fades,
Stretching behind me, a line that defined me,
the stern and the kindly, their faces remind me...
So different, yet similar,
new and familiar,
I look back and see they are looking at me.

All of those faces—
Their gifts and their graces
I seek and I find all their faces combined.
Here is the face of my mother; my grandmother,
staring at me through the eyes of another...
Strength and fragility, toughness and tenderness,
rendered anew and defiantly genderless,
All of those faces—I see every one
looking back at me now in the face of my son.

Those glorious faces—
The faces of womanhood,
Rolled into one and reborn, a new dawn.
No more shades of grey, living colour today,
Born from all of our hearts, you're the sum of our parts.
It's that look in your eye—every tear, every cry
is a rippled reflection of stones that were thrown
long ago; of seeds sown, and regrown...now my own
precious crop turns its face to the sun—
My own son,
Rise and shine, little one,
Women's work must go on.

Amanda Waldron

Eurynome

I am so much more than you know, she said

I am all of creation
I am vast like this world
      I shift shape with the moon
I am the currents of the ocean
I am the love of a mother
I am as unceasing as the wind
I am the call of the wolf
I am the fury of the hurricane
I am the eye of the storm

I call to you like your heart
I am the essence in your blood
I am the unfolding of the butterfly's wings
I am the walls tumbling down
I am freedom in the clouds
      I burn like the stars
I am both dark & light
I am a miracle, always coming to be

I am the spinning of fate

I have my hands in the clay
I am endless like time
I am the scent of the roses
I am the prick of the thorn
      I whirl like a constellation
I am the sea meant for the shore
I am the singer of silence
I am the realization of magic
I am the voice within

I travel in your dreams

I am the blessing
I am the wonder
      I spread like wildfire
I am eternally drumming
I am your true desire
I am the harvest that ripens
I am the joy in a child
I am the bite of the serpent

I am the crest of the wave

I flow like the air
I am wild like the fire
I am the coolness of the waters
  I stand solid like the earth
I am the gentle fall of rain
I am the shadow on the ground
I am the sun on your back
I am the resonance of the song
I am wellness & ease
I am the tireless dance
I am desire incarnate

I am trust both broken & fulfilled

I am the moment of alignment
I am the point of the knife
I am the balance of creation
I am ever expanding
I am knowing
I am the fear in your heart
I am everything you have yet to learn

I am your mirror

I am all you've always known

Paula Wallingford

An ocean within an ocean!

Try as you *may*
It's nearly impossible
To capture the depth
Of this being called *She*
An ocean within an ocean

It's just a splash of the brush
With which Kahlo and Sher-Gill
Repaint the world in incandescent colours

The words with wings
That streak of Plath and Pritam's pen
Rewriting the poetry of the universe

The immense courage
That Joan and Laxmi Bai held
Reconquering grand thrones

Intelligence on par with sexuality
With the sway of Cleopatra and Mohini
Reconstructing power like none before

Or maybe it's just everyday elegance
Of my mother in her shadows
And me with her inherited quiet will
Ordinary lives of extraordinary love

Try as you *may*
It's nearly impossible
To capture the many
Faces of *womanhood*
After all, an ocean within an ocean.

Vaishali Gopal

reflection

always a stranger
looking back from the mirror
but your fresh faces
kaleidoscope my features
returning them familiar

Zoë Gardner

Roots

I look at my face
There's the past
My grandmothers
My Mother
Strong proud Women
With lives well lived
Tales to tell
And so much love to give
There's the present
Me
A Woman
Grateful to Womankind
For paving the way so bravely before me
Giving me choices
I too have stories and love to share
Wisdom to pass on
To my future
There's my Daughter
She's inherited my eyes
Their eyes
I see all the wonderful Women that make her who she is in
those eyes
All our blood running through her veins
Our family tree
Giving her roots that will make her grow
Strong assured and free
Into whatever she chooses to be
Her own Woman

Louise Clayton-Palfreman

Craftswomanship

I grew two new wombs inside mine

XX xx xx

Like Russian dolls they fit within me and　　　　　　　separate
　　　eventually

They are part of a bigger set

An infinity mirror
babushka
babushka
babushka
babushka
babushka
babushka

babushka

many, many female hands
smooth and supple
tired and arthritic
carved and crafted
worked and whittled
and hand painted
each one a unique face

I grew two new wombs inside mine

XX xx xx

　　　　　　　　　　　　　　I am made of a bigger
set

Heather Walker

The Fold

The phrase mad as a hatter
was not from Wonderland
but millinery.
There was so much
mercury in their materials
that hatmakers would
slowly go crazy.

Women wear so many
different hats
you would think
we too could lose
our grip,
but we tip
our hats
to the miraculous,

we are origami alchemy,
with myriad other faces
hidden in the folds;
from all the madness
that comes
our way, somehow
we make gold.

Jem Hathaway

Poem for My Children

I tell them the faces of women
are the moon, reflected everywhere.
In the architect that designed
this house, the builder that constructed it.
The engineer that made sure we have heat,
and light, the farmer that grew our food,
the driver that delivered it. The lawyer
who defends the needy, the judge who uses
their morals respectfully, the social worker
who fights for safety, the company director
and the local veterinarian. The doctor
that diagnoses us, the chemists that create
our medicines, the scientists that work
tirelessly to produce a global vaccine. In
the parents that care for us, in
the authors of our bedtime stories,
the astronauts on the glittering ISS,
the office of the most powerful political
position in the world—one day.

Look closely, for the faces of women
are everywhere
and they are soaring,

Naomi Murcutt

The Faces of the Moon

The moon was my home:
She nurtured me like a mother,
Shielding me from harm in her celestial womb.
She taught me to see beauty in imperfection,
As I grew into a woman under her cratered gaze.
The moon was my ship and my anchor;
Carrying me safely across the ocean of stars,
And grounding me when I flew too near the sun.
Together we weathered the storms that rhythmed her cycles,
She taught me the secret of the tides,
And that to bleed was not a sign of weakness.
When I lost myself in the labyrinth of life
She was my beacon; lighting up the safest path
Just enough to let me think I'd found my own way home,
Her love was unconditional.
So, tonight, as she reaches the apex of her radiance,
Full and godlike in the evening sky, I would like to say
Thank you.

Corinna Board

Where Does Her Light Start?
Where Does Her Light Stop?

The moon, she is the pearl up high,
the salt of the earth puppeting tides.
She collects midnight frights
and beams them back as light.
She waxes and wanes through every phase,
and still, somehow, shows up every day.
Stars shoot, clouds hail, lightening abounds
and even so, she measures the world round.
All of this behind-the-scenes movement
and yet her serene gaze feels steadfast, permanent.

//

Now do you want me to tell you the truth?

She is you.

Michelle K Bengson

A Face That Smiled Always

They said,
Here was a face,
Of a woman,
That smiled always,
So how could this face,
Have a story to tell?

They said,
Here was a face,
That hardly experienced,
The world,
So how could this face,
Write about its ways?

So here is a story
Of a face,
That found its way,
One August day,
A face so loved,
In a controlled space,

A face that was told,
What she must see and hear,
A face that was shamed,
For speaking of its worth,

A face that was deemed too plump,
Too hairy and glum,
Whose lips have been battered,
When she was so young,

A face that was a toy,
That was used and discarded,
A face carved,
With middle names,
'Shy' and 'dependent,'

A face,
Whose voice,
Was sat in a cage,
For so long,
A cage decorated,
With trinkets and thoughts
Of everybody else,

A face, once so afraid,
To force open,
The gates of this cage,
Gates that weighed so heavy,
Under a million pound of judgements,
That were cast its way,

So here is a story,
Being re-written,
Of a face of a woman,
As she begins,
To solidify,
Her broken voice,
As she begins,
To embed and decorate,
Her voice,
With everything that is her own.

Madhushala Senaratne

In the Mirror, Her Face

new   In the mirror, her face somehow looks both old and
at the same time. In some lights, I am reminded of the way she
would
moon   over boys in school. Other times, I only see the soft,
crescent shapes beneath her eyes that beg for rest. I see her years, just
over a
quarter   of a century, a fusion of child and adult. She stares back, with
her
gibbous   eyes that reach into me with
full   transparency and I know I'd do anything for her. Does she see
that she
has already given me the
moon   ?

Jaclyn Sagona

The Faces of Womanhood

like
the sky at sunrise
raging forest fires
gentle streams
rough seas
the moon in bloom
the flowers of spring
volcanoes erupting
volcanoes at rest

they (we; our faces)
are the fiercest, the most
beautiful; even, perhaps,
the very best of
nature's best.

Roxanne Meilak Borg

Artemis

when will we walk the moon
we've selflessly segmented
parts of our illumination
gifted the light to others in
their waning moments
returned to us by another
when our needs are heard
we're all preponderant pearls
to someone, at sometime
we've walked the moon
for we are the moon

Jemma Chawla

All of Her Phases

I am the moon and all of her
Phases—waning and waxing
Through onlookers' gazes.

Sometimes, you can barely see
A hint of me, my energy completely
Absorbed and depleted
From expectations needed
To fulfill, often in goodwill,
Or in the rearing of progeny.

But this gestation of our destiny is still
Phasing through generations
Waxing until man regards us fully,
Not as a fixation
But as a force.

Sarah Munoz

Resting Subway Face

on the subway,
the cars are full of men
and possums curling in on
themselves, eyes fixed
on a page, a purse,
a predator's shoe,
or darting to the doors,
sliding shut,
or closed in camouflage
because surely, playing dead
deters them, right?

this face is just
two eyes glinting
in the glare
of fluorescence
and male fragility.

Karen Sadler

Privileged Woman

I am an incredibly privileged woman
I have only been groped by a store clerk.
I feel dirty and ashamed to ever talk about it
But I have not been brutally raped

I am too sensitive and shouldn't let words bother me
I was only teased for having a moustache through grade school
I felt like I could never be attractive or desired since
But I have not been bullied to the point of body dysmorphia

I am an immoral woman and a distraction to men
I am only told to hide my curves and cover my skin
I feel like I don't have autonomy over my body
But I have not been genitally mutilated

I am an angry man-hating feminist
I am the only woman on my team
I feel alone and like I don't belong
But I have not been confined to the kitchen

I am too demanding and incapable of adjusting
I am only told that I'll have to change if I want a partner
I feel like I will have to squash parts of myself
But I have not been forced into an abusive marriage

I am a serial whiner and complain too much
I am only told to accept the way the world works
I feel like I am a burden and that my needs don' t matter
But I have not been prevented from speaking completely

I am a spoiled ungrateful bitch
I only have to adhere by so many rules and expectations
I feel policed and repressed in multiple ways
But I have not been killed for being born with a vagina

I am allowed to exist
I have more freedom than women of the past
My life is not as bad as another woman's
I am a privileged woman
Therefore, I must be grateful and shut up

Meghana Manusanipalli

Were It Not for Women

I'm not here to captivate you
I'm here to shine a light
On women of the world
To support caregivers
And recognize their hard work
Were it not for women
Across the world and time
Where would we be?
Who would we be?
We celebrate the women
Who care for our health
The community organizers
The creators of new paths
Who see glass ceilings
And walls around them
Yet still find ways to work
Toward equality and peace.

Beth Cusack

Mademoiselle

I exist in the grey
In the shadows between
Colorful lives.

You call me dull
But I am bursting
I am alive.

No room at the table?
I bring my own chair
I bring a throne.

I dare you to
Unseat me.

Jaya Avendel

Woman All The Same

I've been told
I have a serious face,
and also,
you smile with your eyes.
A walking contradiction?
You be the judge,
for I am fierce
and I am tender,
a bite and a brush
of silken splendor,
hesitant to jump,
but enamored of the sky.
I ache for acceptance,
apologize for nothing,
and cling tight to my loves.
I'm flower and stone,
power and femininity,
formed from the earth
with a kiss of divinity.
I'm laughter before
sad love songs,
an abstract to muse,
growing wiser and softer,
tougher and stronger,
but *woman*
all the same.

Catherine D. Miele

Face Me

I don't look the same.
Haven't worn makeup in weeks
Dyed my hair, and my cheeks have filled out.
But you know who I am.
Because the face is just the scene, the cover art
Meant to make you want to lift the flap,
Pull back the curtains to where the actors are.
See the nations I've birthed? See the scars?
The one on my lower belly. The ones in my heart.
The ones on my knees from when I fell in the park.
Remember when I ran from that bar   then raised it?
When I took the apple, was that going too far? When I marched
because we are? *We are.*
I was just doing what I had to do to survive.
To nourish, to feel alive.
Remember when we got in the car and drove and didn't know
the way?
You would have stayed in that goddamn garden the whole day
All the (emotional) labour and the pain and then we get blamed
See how I sustain hope. How I'm filled with love and brightness
and rage.
Will you have the courage to burn?
Will you have the courage to turn and
Face me?

Malgosia Ip

The Faces of Womanhood

the faces of womanhood
are tired of smiling on command.
the faces of womanhood slowly
lace proud with canyons. we'll carve them
how we see fit. we'll carve them
with salt. we'll carve them with lip-
pursed, brow-scrunched, well-
earned anger. we'll call crows to land and stick
to the shores of our eyelids with every
belly laugh. we do not apologize
for convening with birds, bouncing our voices
off the walls. we borrow their onyx wings,
fly to the moon—look how we glow!
the faces of womanhood
are waxing and waning; some days
luminescent, some hidden
in shadow. the faces of womanhood
are lunar: capable of blindness, commanding
tides of earth and hearts of men
from every celestial angle.

Kait Quinn

The Greatest Gift

The greatest gift
I could ever receive
in my life is that
of being a woman.
A woman who possesses
the strength
to live each day
to fight each day
to face new challenges each day
yet thriving...
as women
we break barriers,
we blossom, we bloom,
we set new standards,
we even rule
as queens and goddesses,
sharing the gift of abundance
unconditionally
changing the entire world
one person at a time
and I am glad, I have the powers
buried,
sewed, interlaced,
within myself
deep in my soul,
which I keep discovering,
and rediscovering,
as I rise stronger
every time
I look myself
in the eye
through the mirror,
fulfilling possibilities
of a world, that is yet to
rise and shine
with me.

Noelle Nams

Our Never-Ending Season

"You don't belong" sits in a crease by our eyes
(aged where our mothers stood up for our rights)
kept open to include sisters,
fellow children of the moon,
wise from time spent nurturing generations.

"You aren't strong enough" sets our jaws
(firm where our mothers refused to submit)
above our necks stretched long,
staking claim on intelligence,
ability, determination.

"Your place is in the home" floods our skin
(scarlet where our mothers took charge)
reflected in city office windows,
research lab instruments,
towers of higher education.

"My daughter can... My sister will..." fuels our wild
(bold as a child's braids or Mother's shocks of grey).
Attitude feeds unity, compassion,
our never-ending season
to rise and elevate our situation.

Ann Garcia

She

the world was **heavy**, so **heavy**
& thus the deck shuffled her faces

to reveal a tower of strength
a lover, of **self** & of the **greater**

good, a house of cards forged from the ore
of feminine endurance, a *shelter*

for her sisters & for humanity
in **motion**, **snapping forth**, *perfect, a storm*

of *primal* **screaming**, *swallowing* **violence**
with the most *sacred shattering*

A.i.Firefly

Women's Pantoum

They say a woman should cover her grey
in order to appear more youthful.
She should plump what's too thin
and fill in the lines.

In order to appear more youthful
a woman of forty should dress like she's thirty
and fill in the lines
with thinned ideas of beauty.

A woman of thirty should look like she's twenty.
Youth is prized in magazines
with thinned ideas of beauty
spreading lies of a woman's worth.

Thin is prized in magazines.
Size two doesn't leave room
for the spreading lies of a girl
who sees worthlessness in the mirror.

Size two doesn't leave room
for the weight of deception
seen as worthlessness in the mirror
by the beautiful girl disguised.

For the weight of deception
can only be lifted
by the older woman disguised
as someone she is not.

Ellen Rowland

maiden/mother/crone

maiden mother crone
reduced to the virgin and the whore:
you're the chaste princess
saving the galaxy
in white
or
the princess in dripping gold
sidelined on a forest moon
while your brother and your lover
defeat your father's evil empire

this is the hero's journey, after all

despite old Joe's brilliance
we could only be
either or

but every woman
there ever was
will always be
so much more.

LB Colburn

In My Own Skin

I stare at the faces of womanhood resilient in adversity,
Looking at souls staring at our diversity,
Learning to embrace my own perilous flaws,
As the lines creep across my skin like a tally of scores,
Calculating misconceptions along with imperfections,
Measured by crinkles and dimples making so many
connections,
Allowing growth, honesty, and spirituality,
I look on and reflect baring my own mentality,
Knowing that I'll never be 'perfect,' and to a degree
misunderstood,
Aware that's the beauty of the Face of Womanhood,
Where I wear a perpetual layer of olive tones,
Confidence has been built within these bones,
Sustained to structure, I stand tall,
In life's lessons of the rise and fall,
My eyes are my soul that have witnessed pain,
Blended with millions of shades of hazel, tears in the rain,
Evolving, derived from protection,
My voice unafraid, a discerning reflection,
Sun blushed cheeks, cloaked not covered,
It's not a disguise within myself I've re-discovered,
I am human
A woman
This is no sin,
When I am in nothing—but my own skin.

Tara Aryan

Womanhood Lives

In
Rhythm
the collective beat of birthing dreams

In
Truth
sunrise upon injustice merging a tide of unity

In
Laughter
the curve in our perspective full circle moments

In
Adventure
the unthawing of layers escorting sacred home

In
Persistence
knots on the backs of our sisters

In
Patience
the ride we catch on our breath when nothing is left

In
Life
the web of connection traveling universal light

In
Each other
beacons of resistance
a lighthouse toward the soul of star woven
abundance

In
Womanhood

Melanie DeSumma

Think of a Woman

This woman is a warm bowl of rice, the grain and shape
Of steady even lore. The curve of her voice
A language that exists outside her body

A language that uncoils its golden tongue to disembody
Doubt. The fibre in a rope that binds us to the shape
Of our history. Micaceous face, a raised brow; stories to revoice

This woman leads beyond where hot mouths seek to outvoice
With shrill whistling fear. There will be that, which to embody
Is bowl. Vessel. Briar. But the truth is ours to shape

As women our grain and shape is well versed, warm-bodied,
full-voiced

Lauren Thomas

Matres

Maiden
First steps into this place
where no one holds your hand
and you barely hold yourself
T-Shirts growing tight
mistaken thongs that ride too high
trying to be hot
a long way off.
Skin burned and blemished
from angry hormones and self-inflicted
chemicals that could strip your nail varnish.
Caked in paints two shades too dark
spider leg eyelashes and baby doll red cheeks
from your friend's stash of mum's old make up.

Mother
Chew lips, sometimes sexy, sometimes angsty
mouth in hoops. Eyes clamped, head back
doe eyed adoration for boy, boy, boy
resting bitch face protects from the rest
breathing in and out
through pain, fear, and worship
little hands ask questions
pulling skin, poking eyes
holding in between their paws
staring, drooling, laughing with awe
at freckles, lines, and dimples
sweet sweat pours down cheeks
chasing tears
willing away double chins and baby belly
after years of forgetting
the same girl with the caked face masking acne.

Crone
Lines are dug
feet appear
still the resting bitch face but easier with a smile
that sits lightly on a face that weathered so much
gave a full gaze to loss and love
no waning, no retreat into darkness and absence
a full grin, full stare, full of hell
for a world that wants to look away
give them something to stare at
flutter eyelashes, cake me in paint
lilac eyeshadow and hair to match
remembering the girl you are.

Sophia Isabella Murray

We Are Diamonds

The faces of womanhood
glitter like facets of a
diamond held up to
the light. We dream,
we ache, we bloom,
we make room inside
ourselves for new life—
we sacrifice; colours
gleam at every turn.

We're a soft place
to rest, a warm, downy
breast—even as paie
engraves scars on
tender skin.
Our wrinkle lines
are like tree rings—
revealing age, yes;
but mostly the ways in
which we've adapted
and evolved—time and
experience forging
beauty from our raw,
uncut surfaces.

We emerge,
refined
and authentic.

Our collective force is
the aurora borealis of
Arctic skies—watch as
we applaud and
celebrate one another!

Micah Klassen

The Vulture

Her face was still untouched
by the passage of time and sun.
Crows had not marked the corners of her eyes,
and laughs had not become permanent lines.
She was hopefully tragic,
full of maiden magic,
spending her sovereignty like a trust fund
on silly fools who promised love.
I run my fingers through her long, wavy tresses,
still cleaning up her wounds and her beautiful messes,
all the pain handed down by family and culture,
but now I am the sin-eater—I am the vulture.
I spread my wings like Nekhbet
over the years of my life,
turning corpses and carrion
into sustenance and light,
my blood is transforming
and becoming wise.

Jen Miller

The Faces of a Woman

Imagine a world
where women's faces weren't reduced
to symmetry and proportion; coins stamped
with arbitrary worth:
were for cramming
cock or cunt or cake or kisses into, joyous:
were for looking out of or into,
but not at.

Amy Keelan

Faces of Womanhood

I am an ever changing mosaic
of every woman who has grown
from the roots of my family tree.
a scattering of pieces,
a cloth woven from their threads.

I am a core of iron wrapped in softness,
gentle curves that wear a gown
of grace earned
through trial and time.
an ancient fire that will never dim.

Sare Chafin

The Faces of Womanhood

What if
the faces of a woman
were preserved on pieces
of tissue paper
layered one upon another?
Delicate translucent pages of
exhausted joy
or a roar of power,
taught lips
or a deep smile.

Perhaps these layers
glue together
with tears, sweat, grit.
The more layers
the more the fragile papers
crinkle, crease
fragment.

Maybe you'll never know
the faces of a woman.
Or she may
sit with you long enough
for you to trace your finger
along her jawline
and thumb the edges
of her faces
of womanhood.

Lowri Scourfield

Who I Am

I am Elation
my heart bursts
with the merging colours of my life

I am the Freshness
of the morning dew
I sparkle and melt in the warmth of friendships old and new

I am Fear
not for me but for those around me
my daily life a scene of courageous deeds

I am Sorrow
the imprints of my past
send fronds of grief to tinge my every step—they never last

I am Rage
a simmer beneath a steely gaze can turn to perilous storms
at injustice, neglect, inequality

I am Resilience
like a chameleon I adapt and mould
gentle changes, just to keep afloat

I am Vulnerability
crying at the bus stop for months
knowing and feeling what was coming, irrational in love

I am Tenacity
this petal of a face guards the hearts and lives of those dear to
me
overstep the boundary and you will see another side of me

I am Fatigue
bearing the weight of lifetimes
nursing hearts, wiping tears, grasping tiny hands while love
cradles me in its arms

I am Grace
navigating the pebbles of life
stumbling but not falling; even if I do, the ocean is there to
cushion me

I am
the faces of the women before me
changing my fate and their stories—this is my legacy

Azida Zainal

Babushka

The many faces of womanhood
nest inside each other
Each new face growing around the last
Protecting   Preserving
Interchangeable
Some become worn
They crack and chip
To be repaired and repainted
With each new coat new strength
Others gather dust
Lips purse to reveal faces we once wore
Wondering if they still fit
Each face a phase in time
Each face for a time and a place
Until the babushka surrounds them all
Wise, discerning, containing
Picking through the archive
of faces like memories

Catherine Hamilton

One Womanhood

I've heard it said that we have phases,
us Women.
That we morph and mould and melt
through each fluctuation of our lives.
As Women,
there is a label for each moment in time
and every feeling that is felt.
A marker so permanent that, maybe, the label doesn't rub off.
The ink bleeding, pushing through layers of skin
so that, in reality, there can be nothing else.
The face I see is neither crone nor maiden,
not solely a mother or wholly an enchantress.
This face I envisage, your face, is all of Womanhood.
The one we mirror between us.
The ripple of our footsteps.

Nicola Dellard-Lyle

Mother Earth

The face of womanhood
Is the Earth
A beautifully textured landscape
Of natural imperfection
Across her complexion
The outline of evolution's
Journey through time
Running through the creases
And folds of her skin
History through the ages
Buried in her pores
Wisdom rains down in tears
Warm lashes of sunlight
Streaming from her skies
Her soft caring gaze
Offering droplets of hope
Rays of pure love
To the life she created
Her image reflected
In the elements
Providing comfort on the ground
Strength beneath our feet
Breathing the oxygen into our lungs
Then just holding us
Watching over us
Allowing us our mistakes

Emily Way-Evans

My Face

"i see your aunt in you" they say
i never met her, taken too soon at just 19
a secret i hold in my smile, the shape of my chin

i was a freckled child—now dit dots and rosacea run the show
learned life, learned love
yes, even the parts of me the world finds unworthy

i stopped wearing make up every day ten years ago
i was traveling new zealand
too busy being free to be burdened by an unimportant beauty
standard

now, if i want to wear it, i do
but feel just as desirable without,
this is my face, i am learning to love her so

Sarah Jeannine Booth

Inner Strength

The face of womanhood is often beautiful
Confident and energised
Guided by her inner love
To shine

The face of womanhood is often determined
Robust and resilient
Guided by her inner force
To achieve

The face of womanhood is often complex
Fierce and yet gentle
Guided by her inner compassion
To protect

The face of womanhood is often tired
Weary but unwavering
Guided by her inner strength
To continue

Gerardine Sykes

Contributors

Sifa Mustafa is a London based Illustrator, Designer and Visual Artist who works across a variety of mediums. Her work is often inspired by nature, political and social discourse, music, and her environment.

www.sifamustafa.com
www.instagram.com/sifamustafadraws

Rachel Walker Mason is a multi-award-winning musician and bestselling author, currently writing songs with Grammy winners, Billboard Hot 100 artists, alumni from The Voice UK and American Idol, Emmy winners, and Independent Country Music Association Awards winners.

Named a Woman Of The Year 2020 and hailed "an inspiration" by Prince Harry, Rachel is the only musician to have been crowned Freelancer Of The Year and to be given a Lockdown Hero Award for her work creating the international arts festival Unlock Your Talent which garnered worldwide acclaim for its support and fundraising for mental health.

A highly regarded songwriting and vocal judge, Rachel was a judge for NTA nominated *Sing: Ultimate A Cappella* on Sky One and is a judge for the UK Songwriting Contest, Strive, and the Intercontinental Music Awards.

www.rachelwalkermason.com
www.lyricallight.co.uk
www.listenincolourartistmanagement.co.uk

Zara Al-Noah is a physician associate in the NHS and has two small children. She is happiest in wellies in the countryside and loves to travel. Her poetry was shortlisted for The Folklore Prize and can be found in numerous anthologies. Find her on Instagram @littlepocketpoems.

Lowri Ann enjoys documenting the everyday in her writing. She is a mother to a 3 year old, a teacher, partner, daughter, sister. This piece was inspired by the many roles we wear as women and the beauty in her intricate complexities. You can follow her on Instagram @lowri_ann_writes.

Tara Aryan is a British poet and Indie Author who writes deep, emotive pieces as well as novels. Tara began publishing her work on Instagram and has since been featured in literary magazines and anthologies. Recently, Tara was a collaborative artist for a musician in New York.

Jaya Avendel is a micro-poetess and word witch from the Blue Ridge Mountains of Virginia, passionate about life where it intersects with writing and the dreamscapes lost in between. With writing published at *Silver Birch Press, Rebelle Society,* and *Free Verse Revolution,* among others, she writes at www.ninchronicles.com.

Michelle Bengson is a poet, naturalist, and mother. Formerly an environmental educator for the U.S. Fish & Wildlife Service and now a stay-at-home parent, Michelle's writing bridges the wild and domestic worlds. She writes about nature and relationships—highlighting universal themes of belonging, purpose, and wonder.

Jaimee Boake (she/her) is a high school English Language Arts, Creative Writing, and Leadership Teacher in Sherwood Park, Alberta (Treaty 6 Territory). She loves reading, writing, spending time with her dogs, and is happiest, always, in the mountains. A recipient of the Martin Godfrey Award for Young Writers, more of her work can be found in various literary magazines and anthologies or on Instagram @jaimeeannethology.

Corinna Board rediscovered poetry-writing during lockdown, when she finally found the courage to share her work on Instagram (@parole_de_reveuse.) She recently moved back to the UK from Paris, France and teaches English as a second language in Oxford. She's passionate about nature, poetry and mythology.

Sarah Jeannine Booth is a poet and 3rd year BFA writing student. She finds inspiration for her writing in nature, combined with a curiosity about the pathos of human experience. Sarah lives in Victoria, BC, Canada—the unceded land of the Coast Salish Territory of the Lekwungen and WSÁNEĆ nations. Connect with her on Instagram @sarahjeanninewrites

A lawyer by profession turned stay-at-home mother and a lover of words, **Roxanne Meilak Borg** writes stories in poetry and prose on her blog, A Love for Stories, and on Instagram (@a_love_for_stories).

Adrienne K. Burris is a writer/teacher/mother in Greenville, SC. Her poetry can also be found in *Washington Square Review, Rogue Agent,* and *Mum Poem Press,* among others.

Sare Chafin is a poet and dreamer who resides in rural Maryland in a little house surrounded by trees. Guided by her sense of wonder, her writing reflects a deep connection to both nature and human emotion.

Jemma Chawla is a poet living in Greater London, UK. She finds writing a great creative outlet and much needed form of therapy. Jemma self-published her debut poetry collection *No Walk In The Park* in May 2021. Her work is also featured in various zines and anthologies. @new_stanza on Instagram.

Louise Clayton-Palfreman spent many years treading the boards in London's West End before taking a break from Acting to focus on being a Mum. She exercises her creativity in other ways now and is constantly writing poems, stories and lyrics and continues to share her love of the Theatre through teaching.

LB Colburn is a writer, mother, and village witch who began writing poetry the first time she fell in love, and never stopped. Her work focuses on love, loss, and motherhood. IRL she lives in Northern California with her family, and on the internet she can be found as @motheramongthorns.

Beth Cusack enjoys digging for words, playing with dirt, and repurposing anything else she finds. She is an artist, author, and community organizer living in Texas. She wrote and illustrated the children's book *Making Monster Soup*. Her website is www.bethcusack.com.

Nicola Dellard-Lyle writes poetry and prose on the wilds of motherhood and the serenity of conscious living. Her honest words often reflect deep inner work, realisations, and challenges, whilst weaving in uplifting space for nature and its cycles. Nicola lives with her family in Bristol, UK.

A.i. Firefly was born at the tail end of the 1970s in the suburbs of NYC. She is the author of *Cast Iron Poetry #2 : A Moon Magnetized This Screeching Bird*, a poetry collection published by Time Is An Ocean Publications. Her previous work on the web & in print appears in publications by *Having A Whiskey Coke With You*, NYSAI Press, *Blood Moon Poetry*, A.B. Baird Publishing, *E·ratio,* Train River Publishing, & Great Weather For Media. You can read more of her work and engage with the author on Instagram @a.i.firefly and on the web at aifirefly.wordpress.com.

Karen E. Fraser is a published poet/writer with degrees in Professional & Creative Writing and Anthropology. She utilises the storytelling of belonging and dignity to illuminate truth, social justice, and Oneness. Find her on Instagram @be_nourished

Ann Garcia has a Ph.D. in psychology. Her creative writing primarily explores nature, self, and love. She draws inspiration from waters and woodlands within the Great Lakes region of the USA and her life as a wife/scientist/mother/shutterbug. Find links to her work on Instagram (@solaceinraindrops) and at anngarciabooks.com.

Zoë Gardner is a mother, writer, performer, artist, and mammal native to London, UK. Her visual journaling and poetry is shared as @limberdoodle on Instagram as a form of mutual peer support to record, notice, and value the transition to motherhood.

The soft, raw insides of a woman standing naked with a kind of sincerity that hurts and heals. **Ebony Gilbert** writes what she feels. Her poems are selfies. Unprocessed. No makeup. No filter. Her poetry is somewhat bipolar but then so is she so that makes sense.

FlapperGirlWords is the pen name of amateur writer **Vaishali Gopal**. The name FlapperGirlWords originated from the world of American writer F. Scott Fitzgerald. Vaishali is a lawyer by education, technologist by profession, and lives in India. Find her @flappergirlwords on Instagram.

Catherine Hamilton lives in South London. She has been writing poetry since she was a teenager but recently began to write more as a way of coping with a global pandemic and home schooling. Since then, she has had her poetry published in zines and anthologies. @cathamcreates on Instagram.

Jemma Hathaway is passionate about all things poetry and has performed at various spoken word events around Bristol, UK. Her poems have also been featured on BBC Radio Bristol. She was runner up in Oooh Beehive's national Online Slam Championship 2020 and is the current Hammer & Tongue slam champion for Bristol.

Malgosia Ip is a mother, baker, cocktailer, and writer, not always in that order. Malgosia writes because otherwise, the words would just keep pestering her to get out.

Jessamy Joy is a word weaver who merges matter with spirit into poetry and portals of being. Inspired by nature itself and the nature of existence, she utilizes unique wordplay to create layered poetic tapestries that evoke vivid visualizations while conveying experiences and emotions that provoke thought and expand consciousness. Find her @riverofthegoddess on Instagram.

Amy Keelan is a maker, mother, teacher, and book-lover who lives in the Derbyshire hills (and sometimes runs up them for fun). Her writing is part of a wider practice rooted in exploring stories through drawing and stitch as well as words.

A full time mama of two, **Micah Klassen** began sharing poetry after the birth of her second son as an outlet for processing the beauty and pain of early motherhood. She quickly fell in love with a fast growing online community of fellow mothers and poets and has since had a few of her poems published in various anthologies and magazines. Micah currently resides in Vancouver with her family, you can find her on Instagram @writing_motherhood

Catherine D. Miele lives in Mobile, Alabama with her husband, son, and miniature dachshund. She's found comfort and purpose through writing since childhood and recently rediscovered a love for poetry. She primarily writes about mental health, the complexities of the Deep South (her home), and the ups, downs, and intricacies of life.

Jen Miller explores themes of women's equality, spirituality, transformation, and healing in her prose and poetic verses. Her work has appeared in *Rebelle Society*, *The Urban Howl*, *SageWoman*, and the anthology *Goddess: When She Rules*. Find out more about Jen and her offerings on Instagram @quillofthegoddess.

Sarah Munoz is from Roanoke County in the Blue Ridge Mountains of Southwest Virginia, recognized for its neon star that lights Mill Mountain. She is a mother, a teacher, and a poet. She writes whenever she finds a spare minute. Currently working on her first book of poetry, she is planning on honing her craft and sharing her art.

Sophia Murray is a dedicated teacher, voracious reader, and, above all else, an exhausted mother in the North East of England. Her work combines the spiritual with the feminine because after nearly two years of isolation these are the only two things she remembers how to write about.

Noelle Nams is a creative communicator, published author of 3 books, with her debut poetry collection series "Unconditional" as #1 New Release on Amazon. She is also the founder and editor-in-chief of *Yours Truly Global Magazine*; cultivating a network of inspiring creators. Nams is an IT Professional, Distinguished Toastmaster, social media enthusiast, social activist who loves cooking, gardening, and traveling in her leisure time. To connect, write to her at: inoellenams@gmail.com.

Kait Quinn is a law admin/poet. Her poetry has appeared in

Blood Moon Poetry, Polemical Zine, Chestnut Review, VERSES, and various anthologies. Her books include *A Time for Winter* and *I Saw Myself Alive in a Coffin.* Kait lives in Minneapolis with her partner and their regal cat Spart.

Ellen Rowland creates, concocts, and forages when she's not writing poetry. Her words have appeared in various literary journals and several poetry anthologies. She lives off the grid on a tiny island in Greece. Connect with her on Instagram @rowland.ellen

Karen Sadler (writing under the pen name Kallory) lives in Toronto, Canada with her husband and two young children. She writes about nature, grief, parenthood, and the occasional ghost. You can find more of her writing on Instagram at @kallorywrites.

Jaclyn Sagona is a lover of dogs, plants, hiking, tennis, and of course, poetry. She is happiest when spending time with her husband, family, and best friends at home in New Jersey.

Madhushala Senaratne recently completed her doctoral studies exploring storytelling practices within international development. She writes poetry and short stories and has published both creative and academic pieces. She is a mum of two.

Words have always been **Kara Simmons'** favorite medium. A former journalist who now works as an attorney, she lives in central Iowa with her husband and young daughters. Her deep connection to the natural world as teacher inspires poems, guided meditations, and oracle cards. More about her offerings at www.joyfulresonance.com.

Even as a child **Gerardine Sykes** liked playing around with rhyme, and that hasn't changed. Most of her poems are rhyming—thus her Instagram handle @allsortsrhyme. She is now in her 60s, lives in the Midlands, England, and has two grown up boys.

Lauren Thomas writes about the passing of time, the natural world, and stories told through women's voices. She has recently been published in *The Crank Literary Magazine, Briefly Zine, Re-side Magazine, Abridged, Blood Moon Poetry, Green Ink Poetry,* and *The Mum Poem Press* with poetry forthcoming in several anthologies.

Amanda Waldron was born in the Australian outback and inherited her deep love of words from her crossword-addicted mother. With her catering career largely put on hold throughout Covid, she turned back to poetry as a creative outlet, and her works centre around themes of home, family, and food. Find her on Instagram @adoor_onceopened.

Heather Walker lives in the north of England, a southerner with a northern bloodline. She has a dance degree and an MA in The Body and Representation from Reading University. She works in the culture sector and in her spare time writes poetry and short stories.

Paula Wallingford—living in Toronto, Canada—spends her creative time writing poetry, drawing, painting, and figuring out how she can next express herself. A single mom, Paula has—in no particular order—been a practicing Shiatsu Therapist & Reiki practitioner, a jewellery artisan, an amateur photographer, and currently works in government. You can see more of what Paula is doing (& creating) at @5peony5 on Instagram.

Emily Way-Evans is a mother and production accountant by day and an amateur poet by night. During maternity leave with her second child she took up writing classes with Mothership Writers, a welcome therapeutic outlet during a difficult period of postnatal depression. She continues to keep writing in as many available moments of solitude as possible.

Azida Zainal is fascinated by humans—what moves them, what ails them, and what piques them. She writes about nostalgia and how women face the world. When she is not painting or creating verses, she is a practising ENT surgeon.

Acknowledgements

Thank you to the blood moon POETRY editorial board; Sifa, our cover designer, and Rachel, whose Foreword brings this book to life.

We are also incredibly grateful for our community of poets and, most importantly, the women whose words we publish here.

About blood moon POETRY

blood moon POETRY is a small indie press and a home for women who write poetry. We feature poetry and illustrations by women from all walks of life, striving to support and amplify marginalised voices in particular. Seeking out new and undiscovered creative women, we specialise in the compilation, editing, and publication of print poetry anthologies and pamphlets centred on themes of womanhood. Our bi-annual digital journal also features work from our growing online community of poets, authors, and illustrators. We aim to celebrate the diverse beliefs, paths to, and complex perspectives on womanhood by showcasing that diversity in our publications.

Printed in Great Britain
by Amazon